A New True Book

CARLSBAD CAVERNS

NATIONAL PARK

By David Petersen

CP CHILDRENS PRESS®
CHICAGO

Carlsbad Cavern is filled with
beautiful rock formations.

PHOTO CREDITS
© John Elk III–Cover, 24, 29, 40
© Kent and Donna Dannen, 43
H. Armstrong Roberts–© R. Krubner, 7;
© Camerique, 20
Jerry Hennen–25, 27
Photri–9, 28 (3 photos), 41
Root Resources–© Anthony Mercieca, 13
(top right), 14 (bottom right); © Kenneth W.
Fink, 15 (left), 32
Tom Stack & Associates–© Brian Parker, 2;
© John Cancalosi, 13 (center right), 39;
© Rod Allin, 14 (center), © David L. Brown,
31; © Robert C. Simpson, 45
Stock Montage–11 (top & bottom left)
SuperStock International, Inc.–© James
Israel, 4
Travel Stock–© Buddy Mays, 11 (right), 15
(bottom right)
UPI/Bettmann–10, 16 (2 photos)
Valan–© Robert C. Simpson, 8, 13 (bottom
left & bottom right), 22; © Kennon Cooke,
13 (top left); © John Cancalosi, 14 (top
left); © Wayne Lankinen, 14 (bottom left),
36; © Jeff Foott, 15 (top right); © Stephen
Krasemann, 34
Tom Dunnington–19, illustration; 23, map
COVER: Carlsbad Caverns National Park
cave formations

Project Editor: Fran Dyra
Design: Margrit Fiddle

Library of Congress Cataloging-in-Publication Data

Petersen, David
    Carlsbad Caverns National Park / by David Petersen.
      p.   cm.–(A New true book)
    Includes index.
    ISBN 0-516-01051-4
    1.   Carlsbad Caverns National Park (N.M.)–
Juvenile literature. [1.   Carlsbad Caverns National
Park (N.M.).   2.   National parks and reserves.]
I.   Title.
F802.C28P48   1994
917.89'42–dc20   93-36997
                                          CIP
                                          AC

TABLE OF CONTENTS

Huge rock formations "grow" in the Hall of Giants.

A "DECORATED" CAVE

Have you ever wanted to explore a cave?

In New Mexico, there's a big, beautiful cave just waiting for you! It's called Carlsbad Cavern.

You can hike deep into Carlsbad Cavern on a paved trail. Hidden lights display the cave's strange, lovely rock formations. Scientists call them "decorations."

Decorations hanging like icicles from the ceilings of caves are called stalactites.

Decorations sticking up like fat fingers from the floors of caves are called stalagmites.

When a stalactite from above meets a stalagmite from below, they join and become a column.

Delicate stalactites decorate the Chinese Theater in Carlsbad Cavern.

"Draperies" are cave decorations that look like folds of cloth.

Draperies are wide,
wavy decorations that look
like window curtains. Some
cave decorations even
8   look like frozen waterfalls.

The frozen waterfall in the Green Lake
Room at Carlsbad Cavern

There are no real
waterfalls in Carlsbad
Cavern, but there are many
pools of cold, clear water.

9

An early photograph of Carlsbad Cavern shows
one of the first visitors to the cave.

Carlsbad Cavern is so
big and so beautifully
decorated that President
Calvin Coolidge made it a
national monument in
1923. In 1930, President
Herbert Hoover created

Presidents Calvin Coolidge (top left) and Herbert Hoover
(bottom left) preserved Carlsbad Caverns. Today, hikers
enjoy outdoor desert areas of the park as well as the caves.

Carlsbad Caverns National
Park to protect the cave.

Today, the park includes
46,766 acres (18,926
hectares) of the Chihuahuan
Desert. There are 80 caves,

and in those caves live more than a million bats!

Life of all kinds thrives at Carlsbad. The park is home to 59 species of mammals, including coyotes, mule deer, skunks, raccoons, lots of rock squirrels—and, of course, bats.

There are 44 species of amphibians and reptiles in the park, including snakes, lizards, and frogs.

The animals of Carlsbad include
(clockwise from top left)
mule deer, coyotes, rattlesnakes,
spadefoot toads, and skinks.

Among the many birds found at
Carlsbad are the golden eagle (above),
the turkey vulture (top left),
the black-chinned hummingbird (bottom left),
and the cactus wren (bottom right).

There are 273 species
of birds—from tiny
hummingbirds to giant
14 vultures and eagles.

Flowering desert plants at Carlsbad include agave (left), ocotillo (top right), and cactus (above).

More than 740 kinds of desert plants grow at Carlsbad, including ocotillo, agave, and cactus.

Mescalero Apaches at a tribal meeting. In 1919, when these pictures were taken, the Mescalero Apache people lived on a reservation north of Carlsbad.

And for centuries, the Carlsbad area was home to the Mescalero Apache people.

A CAVE IS FORMED

How did Carlsbad
Cavern and the park's
other caves come to be?
About 250 million years
ago, the Carlsbad area
was not the desert it is
today. It was the floor of a
great inland sea. Slowly,
an ocean reef 400 miles
(644 km) long formed
beneath this sea.
Much later, as the
ancient sea slowly dried
up, the great reef became

buried under tons of ocean sediments.

Finally, about three million years ago, pressures in the earth pushed the buried reef to the surface.

Then, groundwater containing acids from oil and gas deposits below the reef began eroding tunnels along cracks in the reef. Over time, these tunnels became the caves of Carlsbad.

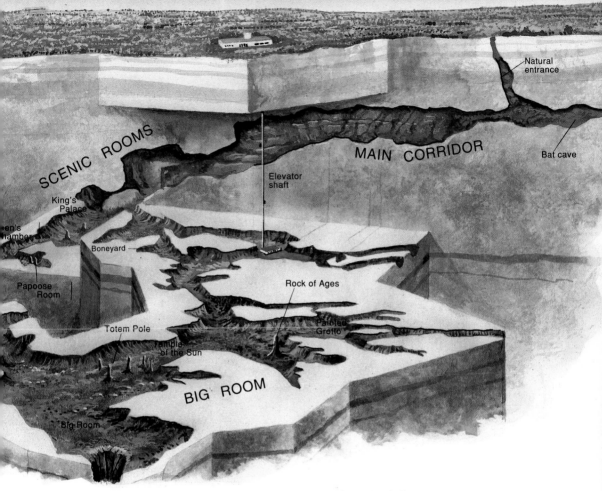

Natural
entrance

SCENIC ROOMS

MAIN CORRIDOR

Bat cave

Elevator
shaft

King's
Palace

en's
hamber

Boneyard

Rock of Ages

Papoose
Room

Totem Pole

Painted
Grotto

Temple
of the Sun

BIG ROOM

Big Room

On the tour of Carlsbad Cavern
visitors walk down the Main Corridor to visit
the Scenic Rooms and the Big Room.

Once Carlsbad Cavern
was formed, cave
decorations began to
"grow." As water soaked

19

Stalactite formations are deposits of the mineral calcite, left behind by dripping water.

down through the limestone reef rock above the cave, it picked up a mineral called calcite. With

every drip of water from

the cave ceiling, a tiny speck of calcite was deposited. As these calcite deposits hardened into stone, they grew bigger and longer. In this way, the cave's thousands of icicle-like stalactites were slowly formed.

Similarly, as water dripped onto the cave floor, calcite deposits built up, and stalagmites were slowly formed.

"Flowstone" deposits are made by sheets
of water flowing down cave walls.

Carlsbad's draperies and frozen waterfalls were formed by water dripping in wide sheets down the cave walls and over rock ledges.

Think about all of this as you explore Carlsbad Cavern. It will make the adventure even more exciting.

EXPLORING CARLSBAD

The park entrance is just outside the tiny village of Whites City, New Mexico. The park road winds 7 miles (11 km) through beautiful canyon and desert scenery to the Visitor Center.

The Carlsbad Caverns Visitor Center

There, you can see
displays that explain how
the caves were formed
and decorated. Other
displays tell about the bats
that live in the caves.

From the Visitor Center,

The natural entrance to Carlsbad Cavern is at the bottom of a cliff.

it's a short walk to the
natural entrance to Carlsbad
Cavern. You can't miss it—
it's a giant hole at the base
of a limestone cliff.

25

Carlsbad Cavern offers two self-guided tours, plus one ranger-guided tour.

The first self-guided tour is called the Natural Entrance route. It follows a steep trail down into the depths of the cavern. Along the way, you will walk through narrow passages and huge corridors filled with amazing decorations.

The decorations here

Left: a formation in the Big Room called the Ice Cream Cone. Top right: a formation in the Queen's Room called the Bashful Baby Elephant. Bottom right: the Boneyard

have names like Witch's Finger, Iceberg Rock, and the Boneyard. When you see them, you'll understand why.

27

At the bottom of the Natural Entrance route, you will be standing about 700 feet below the Earth's surface.

The King's Palace ranger-guided tour begins where the Natural Entrance route ends. From the elevators, this tour takes you through rooms called King's Palace, Green Lake, Queen's Chamber, and the Papoose Room.

At the low point of the King's Palace tour, you will

The Papoose Room at Carlsbad Cavern

be 829 feet (253 m) below
ground!

These two tours—the
Natural Entrance and the
King's Palace—are about
a mile long each.

29

If you're tired by now, an elevator will whisk you back up to the Visitor Center. You can take an elevator back down another day to walk the second self-guided tour, called the Big Room.

The Big Room route leads from the elevators, around the inside of the Big Room (and it is BIG!), and back to the elevators. This hike is 1.2 miles (2 km) long.

Except for Rock of Ages, the Big Room is mostly

The Big Room at Carlsbad is one of the largest underground spaces in the world. Colored lights bring out the beauty of the formations.

level. A large part of this tour is even accessible to visitors in wheelchairs.

This stalagmite in the Big Room
is called the Rock of Ages.

Many people hike the three Carlsbad Cavern tours— Natural Entrance, the Big Room, and King's Palace—all in one day.

And they still arrive back at the natural entrance in time for the evening bat flight.

THE BATS OF CARLSBAD

From a distance, the evening bat flight out of Carlsbad Cavern looks like a swirling cloud of smoke.

Although bats have wings and can fly, they are mammals, not birds. And unlike most birds, bats are nocturnal. That means they are active at night and sleep during the day.

A big, dark tunnel called Bat Cave, which extends a

Mexican free-tailed bats resting on a cave wall

half mile from the entrance to Carlsbad Cavern, provides a daytime bedroom for about one million Mexican free-tailed bats. Visitors are not allowed inside Bat Cave.

Bats sleep hanging

upside-down, packed

tightly together for warmth. At sunset, they wake and fly off to eat. The bats of Carlsbad eat millions of moths, mosquitoes, and other flying insects every night!

Bats use the echoes of high-pitched sounds to locate insects in the dark.

Scientists call this echolocation. When the sound of a bat's shrill chirps strikes something in its path, the sound bounces back, making an echo. These echoes are

Bats have large ears to help catch the sounds that echo back from objects around them.

received by the bat's big, antenna-like ears.

By the different sounds of the echoes, bats can sometimes tell not only how far away an object is, but also what it is and how fast and in which direction it is moving!

Other mammals that use

echolocation are whales and dolphins.

In addition to finding insects in the dark, echolocation keeps bats from crashing into obstacles such as cave decorations, trees—and people.

Are bats dangerous? Well, like all animals, including humans, bats sometimes can carry disease. For this reason, you should never touch or pick up a bat.

When they are left alone, bats are shy and peaceful. In fact, the only bats you're likely to see at Carlsbad are those in the evening flights.

Every summer evening, just at dusk, a park ranger gives a "bat talk" at the cave entrance. Usually just as the ranger finishes talking about the bats, the first wave of bats rises from the black mouth of the cave.

Within minutes, tens of

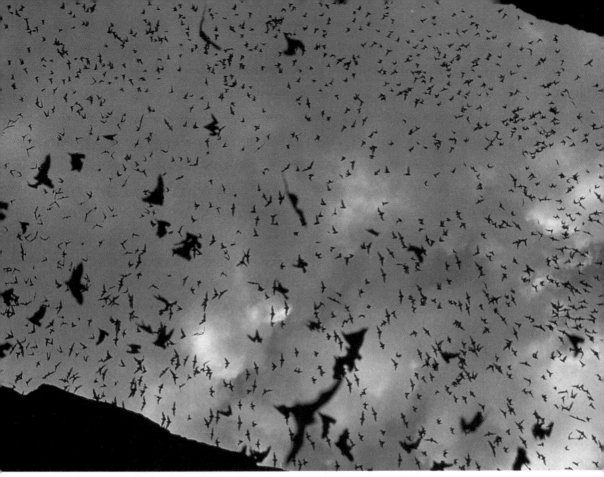

Bats flying out of Carlsbad's entrance at dusk

thousands of bats are
pouring out of the cave
and swirling up into the
evening skies.

You might want to return
to the cave entrance at

Visitors wait at the cave entrance to watch the bat flight.

sunrise to see the bats dive back inside for their day's sleep.

During winter, frost kills the insects the bats feed on, so the bats migrate south to Mexico. It is warmer there, and there are lots of insects for the bats to eat.

40

SLAUGHTER CANYON CAVE

Ancient rock paintings found in the Painted Grotto at Slaughter Canyon Cave.

If you want to explore a "wild" cave, go to Slaughter Canyon Cave. This cave has no paved trails, no electric lights (bring a flashlight!), and no elevators. Ranger-guided tours of Slaughter Canyon Cave are about 2 miles (3 km) long. This includes a steep hike up to the hillside entrance.

41

CARLSBAD "ON TOP"

Back "on top," you can hike the park's self-guided nature trail. It is 0.5 mile (0.8 km) long, with signs describing the plants, animals, and other natural features of the Chihuahuan Desert.

If you're a strong hiker, the park has 30 miles (48 km) of backcountry trails into the desert hills.

You can also explore the Walnut Canyon Desert

Walnut Canyon and the entrance road into Carlsbad Caverns National Park

Drive. This one-way gravel road twists 9.5 miles (15 km) through scenic Upper Walnut Canyon. This drive is particularly enjoyable in the morning and evening.

CARLSBAD
JUNIOR RANGERS

Like most of America's national parks, Carlsbad Caverns has a Junior Ranger program. By completing a fun workbook, you can earn an official Carlsbad Junior Ranger badge.

It will take about two hours to complete the workbook, so ask for one as soon as you get to the Visitor Center.

Carlsbad Caverns National Park is a strange

and wonderful world just
waiting for you to explore it—
both aboveground *and* below.

WORDS YOU SHOULD KNOW

accessible (ack • SESS • ih • bil)–easily approached or entered

acid (A • sid)–a substance, usually a liquid or a gas, that can dissolve other substances

agave (uh • GAH • vay)–a plant with spiny leaves and tall lower spikes

amphibian (am • FIH • bee • yun)–an animal that lives both on land and in water

bat (BAT)–a small mammal that looks like a mouse but has large hairless wings

cactus (KACK • tiss)–a desert plant that has very thick stems and spines instead of leaves

calcite (KAL • syt)–a mineral composed of calcium and carbon; the main ingredient in limestone and chalk

cavern (KAV • ern)–a cave; an underground hollow in rock

Chihuahuan (chih • WAH • win)–the name of a desert in southern New Mexico

column (KAHL • um)–a long, upright structure; a pillar

coyote (ky • OH • tee)–a wild animal that looks like a small wolf

echo (EK • oh)–a sound that is heard again when sound waves are bounced back from a surface

echolocation (ek • oh • lo • KAY • shun)–the locating of an object by measuring the time it takes sound waves to reflect back from the object

erode (ih • ROAD)–to wear away by the action of wind or water

limestone (LYME • stone)–a rock formed by the accumulation of the lime-rich remains of seashells and coral

mammal (MAM • il)–an animal that usually has fur, gives birth to live young, and nurses its young on mother's milk

Mescalero Apache (mes • kuh • LAIR • oh uh • PAT • chee)–a member of the Mescalero division of the Apache nation of Native Americans

migrate (MY • grait)–to travel, usually for a long distance, to find better food or better weather conditions

mineral (MIN • er • il)—substances such as iron, rocks, or coal that are found in the ground

mule deer (MYOOL DEER)—a deer that has long ears and a white tail with a black tip

nocturnal (nahk • TER • nil)—active at night

obstacle (OB • stih • kil)—anything that gets in the way; an obstruction

ocotillo (ohk • uh • TEE • yoh)—a thorny plant with red flowers

reef (REEF)—an underwater rocklike structure formed from the shells of sea animals

reptile (REP • tyle)—a cold-blooded animal that has a backbone and very short legs or no legs at all

sediments (SEH • dih • mentz)—bits of rock or dirt that are suspended in a body of water and then deposited on the bottom

stalactites (stuh • LAK • tytes)—calcite stone formations that hang from the ceilings of caves

stalagmites (stuh • LAG • mytes)—calcite stone formations that stick up from the floors of caves

vulture (VUL • cher)—a large bird that eats the remains of dead animals

INDEX

About the Author

David Petersen first explored Carlsbad Caverns National Park at age eight, and most recently while writing this book. He lives in the mountains of southwest Colorado.